HOOFBEATS, HEARTBEATS & HEROES

ISBN: 1-879234-42-4

Library of Congress Catalog No. 96-078579

Published by Heritage Publishing, Inc., 1720 Regal Row, Suite 228, Dallas, Texas, 75235. Phone: (214) 630-4300

Principal photography by Skeeter Hagler
Additional photography by Francis M. "Frank" Martin, D.V.M., Ron Litt - RL Photo-Graphics and Gerald Crawford

Printed by The Bidal Group

Manufactured in the United States of America

First Printing

DEDICATION

This book belongs to the volunteers
of the Houston Livestock Show and Rodeo—
without them, the pages would be blank.

he story of the Houston Livestock Show and Rodeo is the story of Houston—people of vision taking risks to make a dream come true. The Show, as well as the city, was founded by true pioneers—those willing to look far beyond their own lifetimes to build for a future they could only imagine.

Because of this visionary thinking, a small, unprofitable livestock exhibition grew into an organization that today exhausts lists of superlatives—the Southwest's largest charity, the world's largest donor of agricultural scholarships, the largest and most prestigious livestock show in the world, an unparalleled horse show, the richest regular-season rodeo, an incredible family entertainment extravaganza and more.

The Houston Livestock Show and Rodeo grew because its leaders never stopped looking beyond the far horizon. They never settled for "as good as last year," especially in two vital areas: adding more entertainment bang for the ticket buck and helping more Texas youngsters.

To these ends, the Show has grown significantly every year, adding more glitz and glamour, and expanding and broadening its educational programs. Regardless of the changes and improvements, however, the Show has remained true to its foundations in agriculture and Western heritage, making it a singular experience for its unique combination of rural and urban audiences.

In an era when many of us are at least one generation removed from a farm or ranch, the Houston Livestock Show is a rare opportunity for "city folk" to see cows, horses, sheep, goats and other livestock up close and personal. From the other perspective, rural and small-town visitors get a chance to experience the nation's fourth largest city at its very best. The Astrodome, Astrohall and Astroarena are extraordinary exhibition facilities, and the grounds become home to the most popular musical entertainers, the finest livestock and horses, the wildest rodeo stock and the best cowboys and cowgirls. It's "Go Texan Fever" at its finest.

And although rural themes play a big part in the Show's mystique, it is an event that truly represents the diversity of modern-day Houston. While walking through the exhibits, many languages can be heard, all types of music are played, from country to zydeco to Mariachi to gospel, and almost every kind of food can be found, from Gulf Coast seafood and barbecue to Chinese, Mexican and Italian cuisine.

The Show's supporters are just as varied as the city of Houston, as well. Huge corporations get involved because they know the Houston Livestock Show and Rodeo represents the best of the city's heritage and a key to its educational future. Groups of tiny school children clutching each others' hands, gazing wide-eyed at all the animals and other exhibits, are also an integral part of the Show's support base. From the average working person who supports the Show with a rodeo ticket purchase to the multi-national company that underwrites a rodeo event, the Houston Livestock Show and Rodeo is part of its community.

Visitors to the Houston Livestock Show and Rodeo also see thousands of volunteers, from every part of Houston and from every ethnic and socioeconomic background, working together to make the event the finest of its kind in the world. Some volunteers take vacation and others use their weekends and nights to do their Show work. In return they get a gold badge and a parking sticker giving them the privilege to hunt for a parking space and a seat in the Astrodome, neither of which are guaranteed and are often not available.

Does a small gold badge really drive all of these people to give up their free time to put horses in stalls, dig through trash for cans to recycle, direct traffic and sell advertising, among other duties? It is more likely that the real reason behind the Show's incredible volunteer work force is tied to the rewards immediately following the annual event.

It is after all the excitement ends that the big payoff comes for the Houston Livestock Show and Rodeo. Throughout the spring and summer, the Show awards a wide variety of scholarships to students from all over Texas. These are the best young people in Texas—they are the leaders in their communities, the presidents of their 4-H clubs and FFA chapters, the valedictorians of their classes and the star athletes in their schools. They come from every possible background, but they have a common commitment to excellence that the Houston Livestock Show and Rodeo strives to encourage with its annual educational programs.

Benefiting youth, supporting education, furthering agriculture and providing quality family entertainment—the Houston Livestock Show and Rodeo is truly "the Show with a Heart."

CONTENTS

HOUSTON FAT STOCK SHOW AND LIVE STOCK EXPOSITION

RODEO

SOUVENIR PROGRAM

50¢

RODEO OFFICIALS

Managing Director
Everett Colborn, Dublin , Texas

Rodeo Chairman
W. ALBERT LEE, Houston, Texas

Arena Secretary
FRED ALVORD, Fort Worth, Texas

COLBORN — AUTRY — LEFTON

THE RODEO COWBOYS ASSOCIATION
OFFICERS

TOOTS MANSFIELD .... *President*
EVERETT SHAW .... *Vice President*
CLAY CARR .... *Vice President*
EARL LINDSEY .... *Manager*

Page Twenty-one

JANUARY 31st thru FEBRUARY 15th 1948

The Houston Livestock Show and Rodeo

While the Great Depression had a stranglehold on the nation, squeezing the life out of almost every person and business, seven Houston men gathered to try and shine a light in the economic darkness that had enveloped the Texas cattle industry.

Texans suffered. Scores lost jobs, farms, livelihoods and lives. Many were forced out of their homes, off of their land and into food lines and tent encampments. People searched in vain for work. When it could be found, people would tackle almost any job for food and an extra dollar in their pocket.

During this bleak period in history, the cattle business was a delicate wildflower straining up out of the prairies of the Gulf Coast, but—like everything else caught in the desperate years of the Dust Bowl—it was threatened to be squashed by the hard times. The cattle industry had strong roots. Nearly two million cattle, nationally renowned for quality and superior blood lines, roamed sixteen counties in the Houston area.

However, any promising growth in the cattle industry had been corralled by the fact that there was neither a market nor a processing plant in the region. When ranchers sent their prize herds to market, they shipped the cattle to Kansas City or Chicago. Those who had managed to ride out the Depression found their prospects limited by the confines of the marketplace.

In 1931, seven men who believed in the great potential of the cattle business met to develop a strategy that would help it prosper. They agreed the only way for the Gulf Coast cattle industry to expand was to establish a market and build a processing plant in Houston. Such an endeavor could only be successfully accomplished by establishing the finest stock show that could be organized. That is exactly what James W. Sartwelle, J. Howard West, Julian A. Weslow, W. C. Munn, Marcus Meyer, Haygood Ashburn and W. S. Cochran set out to do.

After intense discussion, the men knew two goals had to be met in order for that first stock show to be a success. First, Gulf Coast region ranchers had to be involved in planning the event. Men from Beaumont, Sugar Land, La Porte, Orange and other communities within the region were designated as directors and given the following marching orders: Mobilize local supporters and get folks to attend.

The second goal was that the stock show had to be a long-term commitment that would continue each year, regardless of cost. As they saw it, they had no choice. Regardless of the financial and economic problems confronting them, "the show must go on," because the future of the Gulf Coast cattle industry was on the line.

The first Houston Fat Stock Show and Livestock Exposition opened in 1932 with little fanfare in a small convention hall built for the 1928 Democratic National Convention. The show attracted only two thousand people and lost nearly three thousand dollars. True to their word, however, organizers quickly raised enough money to pay the deficit and began planning the next year's Show.

Emil H. Marks was not to be confused with P. T. Barnum, but in the history of the Houston Fat Stock

Show, he was the marketing ringleader and his impact on the extravaganza is still felt. Marks was a successful rancher from Barker, Texas, who was appointed as a Gulf Coast director.

In the early 1930s, the Show had no budget for entertainment. Free barbecue was about the only attraction Houston had to put people in the seats. Marks decided a bucking horse demonstration might draw curiosity-seekers to the event. Since he promoted and conducted successful rodeos on his own ranch, finding bucking horses was no problem. The event also would allow Marks to publicize his rodeo and possibly draw a whole new audience to Barker.

After the cattle had all been herded from their pens and paraded before an admiring crowd during the livestock show itself, the bucking horses would explode in a crazed, wild-eyed fury from the chute at the far end of the arena. Volunteer cowboys cautiously climbed onto the backs of these raging dust storms in a battle of grit and gristle, muscle and mayhem, the horses snorting with high-pitched screams, kicking and straining against the ropes held firmly by handlers as stubborn as the unbroken broncs. The cowboys rode spinners that bucked in a tight circle, high rollers that leaped high into the air when bucking, weavers whose feet never struck the ground in a straight line, sunfishers that twisted their bodies into crescents, touching the ground with first one shoulder and then the other, and windmillers that "swapped ends" or reversed their position by making a complete half-circle while kicking in the air. As one rider said of a bad horse, "This hoss swallowed his head and proceeded up to where the lights of Jerusalem shone. There we parted company and the bronc came down alone."

Greased pig races also were staged, where volunteers would mimic the rambling routes of these slippery, pink balls of energy. For a fleeting instant, someone would grasp a piglet, only to have it writhe loose and dart away, bringing more hoots and hollers of excitement from stock show attendees. Show leaders did not overlook the popularity of these events. When it came time to expand the Show, establishing a full-fledged rodeo became a priority.

The Great Depression raged on and ravaged the state. Cattle prices fluctuated. But at the little convention hall each spring, the Fat Stock Show steadily grew. In fact, within five years, it had outgrown its home. City fathers agreed that the old hall had seen better days and approved the demolition of the building and the construction of a brand new coliseum.

Without an adequate venue in 1937, the Show's board of directors decided to invest its efforts in planning the biggest and best event yet to show off the

The Livestock Show and Rodeo was expanded in 1938 to show off the new Sam Houston Coliseum in downtown Houston.

brand new Sam Houston Coliseum the next year. To expand the scope of the Show, organizers knew it was vital to round up help from the entire community. So the Houston Junior Chamber of Commerce, whose members were the Jaycees, was tapped to take charge of ticket sales and the promotion of the event.

The Jaycees were divided into two groups and encouraged to compete against each other to determine who would be able to sell the most tickets. Their goal was eighty thousand. Also enlisted were the Junior League of Houston and students from the University of Houston. These civic groups continue to be recognized for their early volunteer efforts which took the Show to a new level.

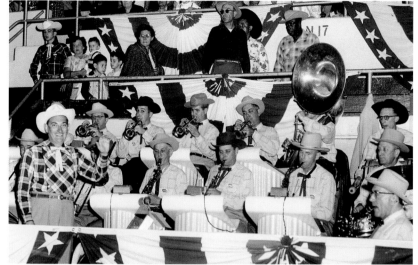

The sounds of music, reflecting the traditions of a western frontier, reached out to attract a broader audience.

To showcase the new coliseum, more activities were planned to attract a broader audience. A parade, a rodeo, a carnival and midway, as well as evening entertainment, were all added to the event. Although emphasis would still be placed on the livestock show—a larger, more expanded version than in 1936—entertainment became very important as the theme "something for everyone" began taking shape.

Staging a rodeo was no easy task. Again, volunteers played key roles in turning the idea into reality. Six men—Joe D. Hughes, Frank Y. Dew, W. Albert Lee, W. B. Warren, Tom Booth and Reese Lockett—donated their time and energy to producing a world class rodeo.

On February 26, 1938, a sharp whistle blast was heard in downtown Houston, setting into motion a solemn, mounted police corps and color guard procession, followed by a twenty-member marching band. Livestock show officials rode horses, trailed by a sixty-five-member cowboy band, along with a drum and bugle

corps made up of area high school marching bands. The Fort Worth Roundup Club rode as special guests of a parade that snaked its way through enthusiastic crowds lining the streets. The downtown parade marked the beginning of the Show and started a tradition still upheld today.

People elbowed their way into the new arena with nervous anticipation. The new structure gleamed under electric lights which hung from the ceiling. Spotlights captured horses and riders, decked out in colorful Western outfits and cowboy hats, as they stepped proudly into the rodeo arena for the grand entry. For many, it was their first glimpse of an indoor rodeo—an event inspired by Emil Marks' bucking horse demonstrations in the early stock shows—and the crowd cheered heartily.

The first rodeo was a theater of chaos and turmoil, played out in a duel between man and beast. The broncs seemed meaner than normal, jumping higher and kicking harder inside the arena. The bulls breathed

The spirit of the old West lived again in Houston.

3

fire. But then, bull riding was a different world. As one rodeo judge said, "The only rule is to stay on. If you're touching anywhere at the whistle, it's a ride." They are, as an old cowboy pointed out, "freight trains with horns." And it took Herculean strength and the balance of a tight-rope walker to remain on the back of a spinning, angry bull for a mere eight seconds, the longest eight seconds known to mankind.

Cowboys rode bulls, as well as broncs, with and without a saddle. They wrestled steers and roped calves, displaying strength and determination, athleticism and uncanny talent with a lasso. The five events included entry fees ranging from $12.50 for bareback bronc riding to $50 for calf roping. Purses ranged from $640.50 for bareback bronc riding to $1,250 for each of the other four events.

The new arena featured a portable floor that was converted into a stage each night and utilized for a vaudeville-style floor show as soon as the dust of the final bull ride had drifted into the rafters. The performance was produced by Kathryn Duffy and called "The Gay Corral Follies." Pretty dancing girls attired in shiny, sparkling costumes seemed destined to touch the roof with their patented high-kick routines. Exotic Spanish dancers clacked their castanets. And musical performers recalled the old-fashioned days of the Old West with their guitars and fiddles belting out cowboy swing.

Outside, a feast for the senses was created along the banks of Buffalo Bayou. A carnival midway featured

Gene Autry rode from the silver screen to become the first national performer at the rodeo.

a fun house stocked with distorting mirrors and a haunted castle that echoed the shrieks and squeals of spooked, but happy, children. Rides spun and whirled along the midway amidst a dazzling array of sparkling lights and cheerful organ music.

The 1938 Show was a milestone that set the standard for all performances that followed. The rodeo and the stock show were forever and inseparably united, while the social service aspect of volunteerism also was instituted, which remains a foundation of the Show today. Additionally, entertainment became an important part of the festivities. The Show had survived the Depression and was now gaining popularity along with the Gulf Coast cattle industry. Its strength would soon be tested, however, with the outbreak of World War II.

The most pressing thought on the minds of many Texans in the early 1940s was the war in Europe. Could it escalate? Would America's sons be pressed into service? What effect would the fighting in Europe and Japan have on cattle prices? Already, construction supplies were in demand and workers who readied the coliseum for the Show were encouraged to be stingy with every nail, board and piece of metal. But through a mountain of hard work and a wealth of good fortune, officials were able to maintain the Show and galvanize Texans for the war effort.

Plans had already been set for the 1942 Show when the Japanese bombed Pearl

Bull riding became the longest and toughest eight seconds ever confronted by cowboys who swore it was like riding a freight train with horns.

Harbor on December 7, 1941, thrusting the United States into war. Show officials hastily called meetings to decide what impact the growing conflict would have on the event, scheduled to begin in less than two months. Instead of canceling the event, however, Show officials decided to dedicate each performance to the war effort in an attempt to give the farmers and ranchers a place to escape from the world's problems.

Nothing spurred the spirits of Texans more than a national hero, and Gene Autry ably filled that role for the first time in 1942. Autry was the legendary radio and movie cowboy crooner of the time. Gene Autry wore the white hat. In keeping with that spirit, Autry sponsored an essay contest called "Why I Am Proud To Be An American," which drew hundreds of entries from Houston students. The winner met the famous cowboy in person and received special recognition at the rodeo.

Autry also led the parade through the streets of downtown, taking over production of the rodeo, adding more style, costumes and showmanship, financing much of the Show himself.

At the rodeo, Dale Evans and Roy Rogers found a frontier wilder than the one they left behind in Hollywood.

The calf scramble, now a staple of the Show, was introduced when local agricultural students were herded, along with calves, into the middle of the arena. Someone yelled "Go," and the calves were cut loose with students in close and frantic pursuit. The object was for a student to corral a calf, halter it and lead it back to the center of the arena.

As one student would jump and grab for a calf, only to be left clutching a handful of dirt, another student would be haltering another calf nearby, only to have the rope halter slip off and the calf bolt away. Should a student be lucky enough to capture a calf and lead it back, kicking and bawling, to the center of the ring, he received a certificate allowing him to purchase a calf, raise it and return next year to show the calf at the livestock show. Since its humble beginning, more than three million dollars in prizes have been awarded, and students, boys and girls alike, have raised more than thirteen thousand calves.

Although volunteers and workers were frugal with construction supplies, even straightening out bent nails, shortages were still prevalent during the war years. Organizers put out the call for donations and again, through the generosity of volunteers, the Show continued, defying all odds. Officials took great pains to support America at war. Free seed packages were distributed so farmers could start their own victory gardens.

Following the war, the Show maintained its steady growth and officials began planning the expansion of the Sam Houston Coliseum. An annex was added, and the horse show was eventually moved to stables across town. However, it would be another twenty years before the Show moved into a new home.

In 1952, Reese Lockett, one of the fathers of the first rodeo, was asked if he would serve again as arena director. Lockett was a successful rancher, mayor of Brenham, Texas, and sometimes described as a little cantankerous.

"I'll never make another trip where I can't ride

home on my horse," Lockett told his lunch companions. One of them, an advertising man named Charlie Giezendanner, jumped to his feet and said, "That's it! If you come by horseback, it would make great publicity for the Show."

So Emil Marks, Pat Flaherty and John Warnasch met Lockett along the old Salt Grass Cattle Trail near Brenham and rode seventy miles to Houston. The Salt Grass Trail Ride gained such notoriety that first year that it quickly grew to hundreds of people hauling their wagons, horses, buggies and mule teams to Brenham to participate. To this day, thousands of riders look forward to participating in the trail rides that kick off the Show.

One of the more prominent names associated with the Show is the Go Texan committee, formed in 1954 and charged with show publicity. Through the years, the Go Texan committees have been responsible for encouraging show-goers to wear western clothing and organizing social events—like the popular dominoes contest and hay-hauling competition.

Always mindful of the future, directors began a scholarship program in 1957 to coincide with the twenty-fifth anniversary of the Houston Fat Stock Show. The program was started to encourage high school agricultural students throughout Texas to continue their education, and shape future Shows in ways that could only be imagined. The first scholarship was awarded to a Houston school district graduate for two thousand dollars.

The School Art Program quickly became a popular event and one of the most visible Show educational programs. Developed for those students who are artistically but not necessarily agriculturally-minded, it started with seven hundred entries and has grown to more than two hundred and fifty thousand participants from seventy-four state school districts. For the first time in 1996, the contest's award-winning works of art were auctioned off. The Grand Champion was awarded five thousand dollars and a total of thirty thousand dollars was awarded to other auction participants. The remaining auction proceeds benefited other educational programs.

In the 1960s, while the world was changing before everyone's eyes, the Show became a constant on which Houstonians could count. But the Show was affected by changes, too. With a nation leaning toward leaner beef, the word "fat" was dropped from the name and the Houston Livestock Show and Rodeo emerged with a new name, but a proud and historic past.

There was no need to be worried about complaints of cramped facilities with the advent of the largest indoor rodeo arena in the world—the Astrodome—used for the first time in 1966. When Judge Roy Hofheinz completed the world's first domed stadium, he said, "I've built a lot of things in my life, but the Astrodome surpasses them all. This doesn't mean it's perfect. But within the limitations of forty-five million dollars, I think it's as perfect as it's possible to be." The Astrodome, referred to as "the Eighth Wonder of the World" has become an American landmark. And when the rodeo was not using the facility, the arena hosted major league baseball and professional and college football, as well as the world's largest indoor crowds for a circus, a fight, a basketball game, a bloodless bullfight and a tennis match.

The structure also signified a new cooperation between Harris County and the Houston Livestock

The parade that winds between the skyscrapers of Houston became the end of the trail.

The construction of the Astrodome in the 1960s signified a new cooperation between the Show and the county, establishing a larger home for the rodeo.

Show and Rodeo. On land close to the stadium, the Show itself financed and built the Livestock Exposition Building called the Astrohall.

But construction was not complete by a long shot. In the past thirty years, seven major expansions have been done at the location with almost all of them financed by the Houston Livestock Show and Rodeo and donated to Harris County. A warehouse addition of more than forty thousand square feet was completed at the complex in 1995, in time for the thirtieth anniversary of the Show at the Astrodome. To date, the replacement costs of the Show's contribution to the facilities at the complex exceeds $125 million.

Perhaps the Astrodome was not properly christened until royalty visited, and, in 1970, Elvis Presley himself entered the building, drawing 43,614 screaming fans for one concert—a record that would stand for eight years. Presley's participation was another milestone, much like Gene Autry's performances nearly thirty years before. It set the stage for nationally renowned performers who would entertain a new generation of rodeo fans.

Continuing its allegiance to education in 1971, the Houston Livestock Show and Rodeo gave one hundred thousand dollars in grant money to three schools: Stephen F. Austin State University, Sam Houston State University and East Texas State University for research projects on the breeding and feeding of cattle. Since the start of this program, over $4.7 million in research grants have been awarded to

when Elvis Presley entertained in the Astrodome in 1970, the rock 'n' roll legend set an attendance record of 43,614 fans.

ten state schools.

Because barbecue and Texas are virtually synonymous, the first World's Championship Bar-B-Que Contest was conducted in 1974, and remains a constant staple of the Show today. Last year, 305 entries each supplied at least sixty pounds of brisket, dishing it up to spectators who roll up their shirtsleeves and chow down in rhythm to the music and songs coming from a nearby stage.

A huge boost to live entertainment at the Show came in 1986 when a high-tech portable stage was added to the Astrodome. Outfitted with new lighting, the latest electrical and sound equipment, plus a turntable and wheels that allow it to be moved to and from the middle of the rodeo arena, the new platform was built to help meet the staging requirements of modern performers. On February 23, 1996, George Strait drew the Show's largest crowd of 62,936, breaking Garth Brooks' three-year-old record attendance mark

by 218. Country and Western entertainers such as Alan Jackson, Clint Black, Reba McEntire and Alabama, plus such popular artists as Emilio, Gladys Knight and Kool & the Gang continue to pack in the crowds.

To find out where the Houston Livestock Show and Rodeo is going, consider where it has been. From an original committee of seven men, the event has grown to nearly twelve thousand volunteer workers involved with ninety-three committees in 1996. Four men rode the Salt Grass Cattle Trail for the first time to the Show in 1952, while more than six thousand riders traversed fourteen different cattle trails leading to Houston in 1996. Some riders even followed the Los Vaqueros Rio Grande Trail, 386 miles from Hidalgo, Texas.

Numbers from the 1997 Show include: a total general attendance of 1,788,437; a rodeo prize purse of $700,758; World's Championship Bar-B-Que attendance of 145,973; more than one million dollars in proceeds generated from the carnival and more than seven million dollars in auction sale totals.

The parade included six thousand horses, eleven bands, twenty-four floats, five enormous balloons and numerous wagons, a far cry from the original 1938 parade that included less than one hundred riders and three bands.

The Houston Livestock Show and Rodeo was born out of the desperation of the Great Depression. It cut its teeth on the hardships of war, steadily growing, but always mindful of the ideals set forth by its founders. The state cattle and agricultural industries have prospered and the future is assured through a strong, unwavering commitment to benefit youth and education. The 1997 Show marks the sixty-fifth anniversary and much has changed, but the Houston Livestock Show and Rodeo remains a constant each year like the changing of seasons.

More than six thousand trail riders followed fifteen different trails on their journey to Houston.

The early mist of a February dawn filters slowly through the forests as trail riders awaken and prepare for another day on rich Texas soil.

The chilled morning echoes with the sounds of wagon wheels and horseshoes clattering along an open roadway. A long line of trail riders gather once more to capture the past.

Riders depart at sunrise
amidst shadows of
brush and trees in an
unspoiled land and
press on toward the city
that awaits them.

Thousands gather as the annual rodeo run winds its way gloriously through the streets of downtown Houston.

Since 1938, the opening of the Houston Livestock Show and Rodeo has been ushered in by a parade. The colorful floats, costumed riders and horse-drawn wagons offer a glimpse of Houston through the ages.

The parade lives and rides
forever in the faraway eyes
of a child.

The streets of Houston are filled with the pomp and circumstance of college and high school bands that march on to a beat as strong and as vibrant as the heartbeat of the Show itself.

It never lasts long enough.
All of Houston smiles with
pride when the parade
passes by.

Since 1974, cooks from around the globe have been concocting their own versions of the unofficial state dish of Texas during the Show's World's Championship Bar-B-Que Contest. More than three hundred cowboy chefs hover around the homemade pits, mixing up their special recipes, while musicians cut loose on Western swing and dancers two-step in nearby tents.

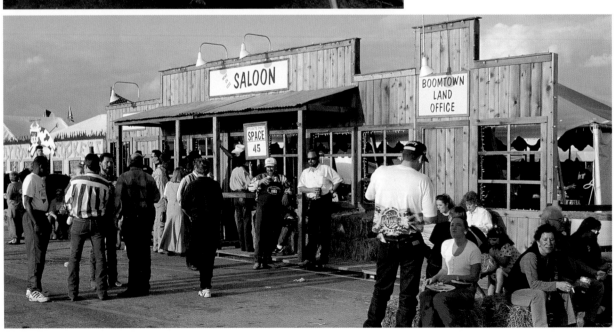

Amidst a backdrop of covered wagons and Western saloons, they cook up a minimum of sixty pounds of beef, ribs or chicken and go to great lengths to protect their secret recipes.

It is an entry as grand as its name. The air is electric. The pulse quickens. The duels between man and beast are about to begin.

The action of the rodeo is a wild, frantic backdrop to the memorable stage performance of Wynnona, an entertainer who can be playful on stage one moment, then wring your emotions dry the next.

"When I climb over that chute and sit down in there, well, I've done it hundreds of times before. I just sit down and relax. It's me an' him. The eight seconds go fairly quick if you're havin' no trouble. But if he has you in a storm and his head in the dust, those eight seconds can last all night."

"He swallowed his head and
proceeded up to where the
lights of Jerusalem shone.
There we parted company, and
the bronc came down alone."

As the rodeo announcer says, when it comes to bareback bronc riding, "It's not how big the cowboy is, it's how much cowboy the Good Lord has stuffed into a pair of boots."

Brooks and Dunn
weave their stories
of life in the
words of a song.

For team ropers,
success takes talent,
skill, determination
and the uncanny
ability to put
complete faith in
their horses and
their partners.
Being lucky never
hurts, either.

Each night, twenty-eight boys and girls chase a dream. They run, grab, hang on, lose their grip, get up, dust themselves off and leap again at the fourteen calves running wild in the four-acre Astrodome arena. The ones that halter a calf win a $1,000 certificate, good for the purchase of a registered beef or dairy heifer. More often than not, the dreams kick back.

The Astrodome reverberates
to the country hits of Reba
McEntire, who, as a young
girl, learned all about the
agony and ecstasy of rodeo
competition astride her
barrel racing horse.

They stand calmly, thousands of pounds of
explosives in hide and horn. The cowboys and
cowgirls of the rodeo may be the stars, but
they speak softly with pride, admiration and
respect for the stock that awaits them.

cowboys fight their nerves.
They have one chance, and
the chance only lasts for
eight seconds. The moment
of their ride nears. It can't
come soon enough. On some
nights, they would rather
put it off forever or until
their nerves quit churning
in the pits of their bellies.
They never do.

RODEO

There is speed and a rare understanding between cowgirl and horse as they attack the barrels, cutting every corner, saving every second, racing an unforgiving clock that never gives any of them a break.

Alan Jackson sings of a heartbroken life
known only too well by bull riders caught in
the eye of a hurricane with horns.

The funny faces are dead serious. The life and limbs of bull riders depend on them, the clowns in grease paint and baggy pants, the athletes who must outrun, outjump and outfight a bull, if necessary, to give the rider time to crawl from the eye of the storm.

As one cowboy said, "Winnin' is gettin' off in one piece." Clay Walker
had the same feeling when he began his career singing in the
honky tonks of East Texas.

George Strait feels at home with rodeo. A skilled
team roper, he sponsors a team penning and roping
competition at his ranch each fall. And during the
1996 Houston Livestock Show and Rodeo, George
Strait welcomed his millionth fan as a solo
performer. Strait truly symbolizes Texas and the
Texas sound. He is an entertainer who has stuck to
his brand of down-home country music with a few
nods toward the traditions of Texas swing.

Cowboys and cowgirls have always been proud of their cutting horses. As one said of his mount, "He could cut the baking powder out of a biscuit without breaking the crust."

Nowhere is more money paid out than at the Houston Livestock Show. It holds the world's records for prices paid for champion animals. In 1995, the Grand Champion Steer of the Junior Show walked out of the Astroarena with a half-million-dollar price tag. The Livestock Show financially rewards many students, but no reward is greater than standing tall and knowing you've done your best in Houston.

They come from every corner of Texas. They have devoted so many hours and so much hard work in barns and pastures and backyards. Some leave with trophies, some with cash. But all are part of a legacy that earmarks a champion.

Days and weeks and months of hard work all end so quickly. A nod. The number. The final word from the auctioneer. And the animal belongs to someone else. Many college educations are earned this way.

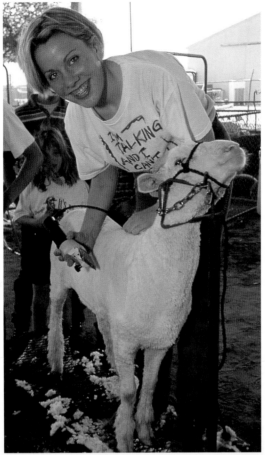

The day is devoted to lambs and the students who raised them, investing so much of their time to make them champions. All are winners. But only one can win. The day may begin with frowns of tension, but it ends with a smile.

The heritage of
Texas may have
been founded in
cattle and horses,
but the soil of Texas
ranch land now bears
the unmistakable
print of llamas. It's
a new day and a
new Texas.

There's a time to work, a time to show, a time to buy and a time to rest.

The Texas legacy of fine horses was underscored by the essayist who wrote, "wherever a man has left his footprint in the long ascent from barbarism to civilization, we will find the hoofprint of the horse beside it." In Houston, the hoofprint of horse stands side by side with the bootprint of the young.

For a time, ever so brief, the West is as wild as it once was. Jerry Díaz performs as the traditional charro of Hispanic culture. Max Reynolds, the Roman Rider, thunders past on horseback. And the Wacky Women of the West are featured in a rope-spinning exhibition.

SPECIAL ATTRACTIONS

The midway is a reflective splendor of Ferris Wheel lights. Exhibitions and special attractions on the grounds are a montage of sight and sound, sometimes untamed and foreign. The Mariachi trumpets are enjoyed by people of diverse cultures.

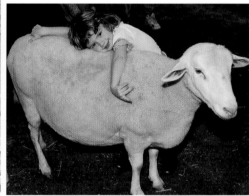

For the young, it's a Never-Never Land, a chance to take home memories of a lifetime.

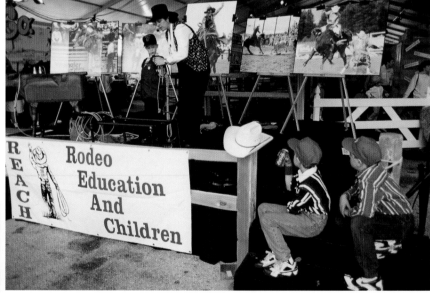

"I come from a little town of 350 people.
My hometown would fit in the Astrodome."

Houston Rodeo Cowboy

POINTS OF INTEREST
FACTS AND FIGURES THAT MAKE THE HOUSTON LIVESTOCK SHOW AND RODEO
LIKE NO OTHER CHARITY IN THE WORLD

Number of volunteer committees	92
Number of volunteers	11,444* (approximate)
Houston Livestock Show and Rodeo membership	31,750* (approximate)
Annual education commitment	more than $4 million
Total auction sales	$7,382,934 (1997)
Record total general attendance	1,830,265 (1996)
Date of first livestock show	April, 1932
Number of visitors to first livestock show in 1932	2,000
First satellite link to space for live conversation with astronauts	Columbia Space Shuttle, March 2, 1996
Record rodeo purse	$700,758 (1997)
Number of years in the Astrodome	31
Total amount of educational support provided to Texas students since first scholarship was awarded in 1957	$46,726,168 (as of 1997)
Educational commitment for 1997-1998 school year	$4.37 million
First Star Trail inductees	Roy Rogers, Gene Autry and George Strait
Number of seats in the Astrodome for Houston Rodeo configuration	58,172
Number of horse show entries	9,679 (1997)
Number of commercial exhibitors	333 (1997)
Number of 4-year $10,000 scholarships awarded in metropolitan scholarship program	120 (1997)
Number of livestock and horse show entries	33,367 (1997)
Number of horses ridden in downtown rodeo parade	6,000 (approximate)
First school art auction	1996 ($254,900 in sales)
Number of horses in horse show	3,299 (1997)
Price paid for first Grand Champion Steer in 1932	$504
The only year no livestock show was held	1937 (the Sam Houston Coliseum was being built)
The year of the first rodeo and downtown rodeo parade held in conjunction with the livestock show	1938
The show's first "star" entertainer	Gene Autry - "The Singing Cowboy"
The year of the first "star" entertainment	1942

The first calf scramble event	1942
The first Salt Grass Trail Ride	1952
Number of riders on the first Salt Grass Trail Ride	4
Origination of first Salt Grass Trail Ride	Brenham, Texas
Number of trail riders in 1997 trail ride	6,000 (approximate)
The year of the first rodeo parade	1938
The year the original Houston Fat Stock Show and Livestock Exposition changed its name to the Houston Livestock Show and Rodeo	1961
The first year the Houston Rodeo was held inside the Astrodome	1966
Amount of first major educational scholarship	$2,000
The first year a major educational scholarship was awarded	1957
The year a research program commitment of $100,000 annually was launched to support research studies in various Texas colleges	1971
Entertainer holding individual performance attendance record from 1970-1978	Elvis Presley
The year of the first World's Championship Bar-B-Que Contest	1974
The year the show expanded its 4-year scholarship program to include students in the Houston metropolitan area	1989
The year of the first pay-per-view television broadcast	1994
Minimum quantity of meat required for competing in the World's Championship Bar-B-Que Contest	60 pounds
The year the first Go Texan Committee was formed	1954
Number of bales of hay required to load in the Go Texan Hay Hauling Competition	42 bales - men 28 bales - women
Replacement cost of Astrohall and Astroarena— facilities built and paid for by Houston Livestock Show and Rodeo	$125,000,000 (approximate)
Number of rodeo tickets available for sale	1,163,440 (1997)
Amount of money generated throughout the world annually by the show	$250,479,933 (computed with economic multipliers from direct expenditures of $84,080,395 as of 1989)
Number of Go Texan Contests	7 (dominoes contest, hay hauling competition, horseshoe pitching contest, photography contest, quilt contest, team penning competition and washer pitching competition)
Number of runners in the annual Conoco 10K Rodeo Run	5,000 (approximate)

* As of end of 1997 Show

Length of the annual Conoco 10K Rodeo Run	6.2 miles
Required measurement of rodeo parade float frame or platform	8 feet by 12 feet
Number of trail rides culminating in downtown rodeo parade	15 different rides
Longest distance traveled by trail riders to Houston for rodeo parade	386 miles from Hidalgo, Texas (Los Vaqueros - Rio Grande Trail Ride)
Benefit of typical show's recycling efforts	17.9 tons of recycled cardboard; 11.3 tons of recycled glass; 15.6 tons of recycled aluminum (1997)
Record number of foreign countries represented at Show	75 (1996)
Length of pig race track	150 feet
Number of questions on the State FFA Tractor Mechanics Contest written test	100
Horse show prize money	$263,293 (1997)
Number of seats in the Astroarena	6,000
Maximum hair length of junior market steers	$1/4$ inch (excluding tail switch)
Number of judging contests offered by the show	8
Number of open show cattle sales in 1997	13
Number of junior livestock auctions	4 (steer, poultry, lamb, swine)
First president of the Houston Fat Stock Show and Livestock Exposition	James W. Sartwelle (1932-1948)
First year the show offered annual memberships	1938
Cost of annual show membership in 1938	$5.00
First female director of the show	Wilhelmina Beane (1938)
The first year Roy Rogers, "King of the Cowboys", and his wife, Dale Evans, "Queen of the West", entertained at the rodeo	1950
The year the guaranteed auction premium program was implemented	1994
Time a cowboy is required to ride in bull riding competition	8 seconds
Number of calves in a single calf scramble	14
Total dollar amount of calf scramble competition awards since inception of the event in 1942	$5,033,000
Number of participants in a single calf scramble	28 boys and girls
Amount of award of calf scramble winner	$1,000 certificate for purchase of registered beef or dairy heifer
Number of animals raised by winners of the calf scramble competition	14,236
First entertainer to perform for one million total Houston rodeo fans	Charley Pride
Number of teams per race in the miniature chuck wagon races	3
First year of Exceptional Rodeo	1986
Number of endowments at Texas colleges and universities	39 (as of August 1996)
Number of Texas universities sharing in approximately $150,000 annually for research programs	10 (amount to each university varies)

Number of school districts represented in the school art program	74
Number of entries in the school art program annually	250,000 (approximate)
Record total attendance at the World's Championship Bar-B-Que Contest	176,184 (1996)
Number of scholarship awards given to Texas students since 1957	16,000 (approximate)
The entertainer who broke all Houston Rodeo attendance records	George Strait (February 23, 1996)
The year the sale of Houston Livestock Show and Rodeo life memberships was approved	1953
Number of rodeo competition events sanctioned by Professional Rodeo Cowboys Association and the Women's Professional Rodeo Association at the Houston rodeo	7 (bareback bronc riding, barrel racing, bull riding, calf roping, saddle bronc riding, steer wrestling and team roping)
Total sales at junior show auctions	$4,636,124 (1997)
Number of presidents of the Houston Livestock Show and Rodeo during its 65-year history	18
Date the Houston Livestock Show and Rodeo hosted a "Texas Rodeo and Grand Ole Opry" for the leaders of the industrialized nations attending the Economic Summit of Industrialized Nations	July 8, 1990
World record price for Grand Champion Steer	$500,000 (1995)
World record price for Reserve Grand Champion Steer	$195,000 (1997)
World record price for Grand Champion Turkey	$67,000 (1995)
World record price for Reserve Grand Champion Turkey	$65,000 (1993)
World record price for Grand Champion Pen of Broilers	$80,000 (1995)
World record price for Reserve Grand Champion Pen of Broilers	$45,000 (1993)
World record price for Grand Champion Barrow	$85,000 (1997)
World record price for Reserve Grand Champion Barrow	$41,000 (1995)
World record price for Grand Champion Lamb	$130,000 (1997)
World record price for Reserve Grand Champion Lamb	$63,000 (1997)
Price paid for the record auctioned Grand Champion piece of artwork in the School Art program	$100,000 (1997)
Largest number of cooking spaces in the World's Championship Bar-B-Que Contest	324 (1997)
A six-time All-Around World Champion Cowboy, the first rodeo competitor to be Grand Marshal of the downtown rodeo parade	Ty Murray